My Monster Friends

Some of my best friends are monsters. They help me whenever I need a hand.

My first monster friend is as tall as a flagpole.

4

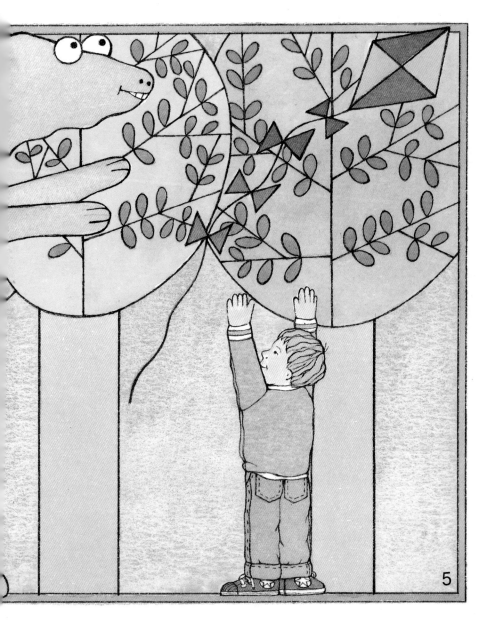

5

He gets my kite down when it's stuck in a tree.

6

My second monster friend has
a brain like a computer.

He helps me do my homework.

8

My third monster friend has hands
like magnets.

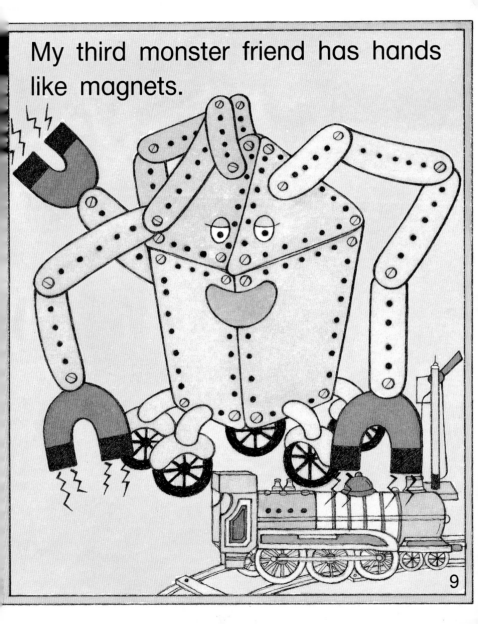

He helps me clean up my room.

My fourth monster friend has
a mouth like a vacuum cleaner.

He helps me clear away the leaves.

My fifth monster friend has eyes like flashlights.

He helps me see in the dark.

Some of my best friends
are monsters.

Could you use a monster friend, too?